THIS LAND CALLED AMERICA: **PENNSYLVANIA**

CREATIVE EDUCATION

Published by Creative Education
P.O. Box 227, Mankato, Minnesota 56002
Creative Education is an imprint of The Creative Company
www.thecreativecompany.us

Design by Blue Design (www.bluedes.com)
Art direction by Rita Marshall
Book production by The Design Lab
Printed in the United States of America

Photographs by Alamy (brt PHOTO, ClassicStock, H. Mark Weidman
Photography, Tom Till, Vintage Images), Art Resource (Erich Lessing),
Corbis (Bettmann, Burstein Collection, Matt Campbell/epa, W. Cody, Lynn
Goldsmith, Richard T. Nowitz, Reuters, David Jay Zimmerman), Dreamstime
(Searchlightphotos, Wolfgang64), Getty Images (Peter Gridley, Kean Collection,
Library of Congress, Mark S. Wexler), iStockphoto

Library of Congress Cataloging-in-Publication Data
Gunderson, Jessica.
Pennsylvania / by Jessica Gunderson.
p. cm. — (This land called America)
Includes bibliographical references and index.
ISBN 978-1-58341-791-1
1. Pennsylvania—Juvenile literature. I. Title. II. Series.
F149.3.G86 2009
974.8—dc22   2008009517

First Edition
9 8 7 6 5 4 3 2 1

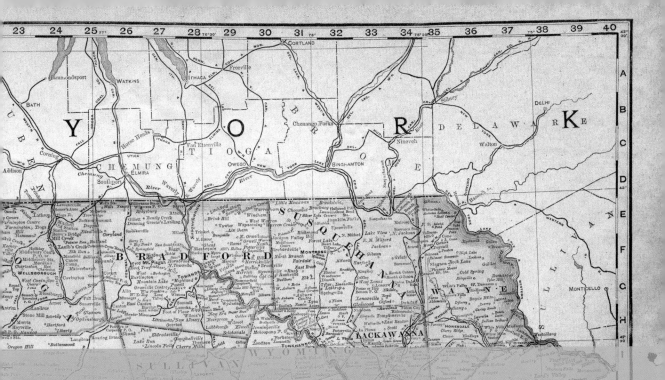

This Land Called America

PENNSYLVANIA

Jessica Gunderson

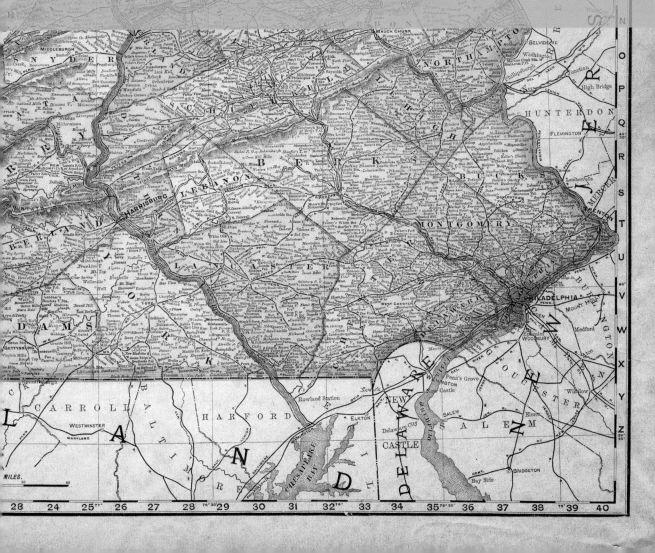

THIS LAND CALLED AMERICA

Pennsylvania

JESSICA GUNDERSON

INSIDE PHILADELPHIA'S INDEPENDENCE PARK, VISITORS WANDER IN AWE. THEY ARE WRAPPED IN A CALM SILENCE. THE TOURISTS FEEL AS IF THEY HAVE STEPPED BACK IN TIME TO THE EARLY COLONIAL DAYS OF THE 1700S. AHEAD, THE BELL TOWER OF INDEPENDENCE HALL RISES INTO THE SKY. THIS IS WHERE MEN SIGNED THE DECLARATION OF INDEPENDENCE AND THE CONSTITUTION OF THE UNITED STATES OF AMERICA. AFTER TOURING THE HALL, PEOPLE MAKE THEIR WAY TOWARD THE PLACES WHERE GEORGE WASHINGTON, BENJAMIN FRANKLIN, AND BETSY ROSS ONCE LIVED. A TRIP TO HISTORIC PHILADELPHIA CONVINCES EVERY VISITOR THAT THIS WAS TRULY THE BIRTHPLACE OF A NATION.

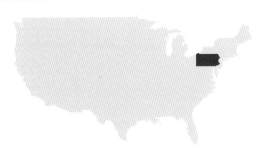

YEAR

1609   Henry Hudson sails up the Delaware River and lands in Pennsylvania.

EVENT

America's Birthplace

Before Europeans settled in the land that would become Pennsylvania, many American Indian tribes lived along the region's rivers and lakes. The Delaware, Susquehannock, and Erie all made their homes in different parts of the state. These tribes fished, hunted, and farmed.

In 1609, Englishman Henry Hudson became one of the first Europeans to set foot in Pennsylvania. He worked for the Dutch East India Company. Hudson's explorations helped the Dutch control European trade with the American Indians. In 1638, the Swedish began settling the area and trading with the Indians as well. They called the area New Sweden. But in 1655, a Dutch army claimed New Sweden as part of their New Netherland territory.

Then in 1664, New Netherland became a colony of England. Part of the colony was given to William Penn and named Pennsylvania, which means "Penn's Woods." Penn was a Quaker. Quakers were religious people who practiced peace and kindness. Penn welcomed Quakers to Pennsylvania. He also welcomed people of different faiths.

Penn believed in freedom for all. He signed treaties, or peace agreements, with the Indians. For many years, the colonists

Although William Penn bought land peacefully from the Indians (above), by the 1900s, most tribes (opposite) had been driven from the state.

1681 King Charles II grants land to William Penn, who gives the area the name Pennsylvania.

State bird: ruffed grouse

and Indians lived side-by-side in peace. But as more Europeans settled in the area, the Indian tribes were pushed west.

Penn set up a town called Philadelphia along the Delaware River. People flocked to the new city. One of these people was Benjamin Franklin. He first came to Philadelphia in 1723 and opened a printing shop five years later. Franklin became a great scientist, inventor, and thinker. His successful printing press made Philadelphia the publishing center of the colonies.

The words printed in Philadelphia helped fuel the American Revolution. The colonists were angry about having to pay high taxes to England. A group of colonial leaders met in Philadelphia to discuss the problem. Before the Revolutionary War broke out in 1775, these leaders decided that the colonies should be free of England's rule. They signed the Declaration of Independence at Philadelphia's State House (later renamed Independence Hall) on July 4, 1776.

Leaders, called delegates, from the 13 colonies met in Philadelphia to make decisions about the Revolutionary War, finances, and government. After the colonists won the war, the United States' Constitution was written at the State House. Pennsylvania's delegates signed the Constitution on December 12, 1787, making Pennsylvania the second state. Philadelphia served as the U.S. capital from 1790 until 1800.

Benjamin Franklin published the famous book Poor Richard's Almanack *at his Philadelphia shop.*

YEAR

1731   Benjamin Franklin opens the nation's first lending library in Philadelphia.

EVENT

It took Abraham Lincoln about two minutes to recite the Gettysburg Address on November 19, 1863.

Pennsylvanians were among the first to oppose slavery. In 1780, Pennsylvania officially outlawed slavery in the state. Later, the state became an important stop on the Underground Railroad, a system of hiding places for runaway slaves.

The American Civil War, a conflict between Northern and Southern states, began in 1861. An important battle was fought in Gettysburg, Pennsylvania, in 1863. After the battle, President Abraham Lincoln gave a famous speech called the Gettysburg Address, in which he declared that the war was being fought for the freedom of all people.

When the Civil War ended, Europeans poured into Pennsylvania to work in the state's steel mills, coal mines, and factories. In 1873, a man named Andrew Carnegie opened the country's first steel plant near Pittsburgh. The production of steel was important to the state's economy, and Pennsylvania remained a top industrial state well into the 20th century.

Andrew Carnegie made a fortune from the steel produced in the many factories he owned.

YEAR

1776   On July 4, the Declaration of Independence is signed in Philadelphia.

EVENT

Mountains and Forests

PENNSYLVANIA IS KNOWN AS A MID-ATLANTIC STATE,
EVEN THOUGH IT DOESN'T TOUCH THE ATLANTIC OCEAN.
THE STATE IS SHAPED LIKE A RECTANGLE. ITS EASTERN
BORDER IS CURVED AND FOLLOWS THE DELAWARE RIVER.
ACROSS THE RIVER LIES NEW JERSEY. NEW YORK MAKES
UP MOST OF PENNSYLVANIA'S NORTHERN BORDER. LAKE
ERIE, ONE OF THE GREAT LAKES, ALSO TOUCHES 40 MILES

(64 km) of the state's northern boundary. Ohio borders the state to the west, and West Virginia is to the southwest. Maryland and Delaware share Pennsylvania's southern border.

Pennsylvania's land is divided into seven regions. The regions of the Appalachian Ridge and Valley, the Allegheny Plateau, and the Piedmont cover most of the state. The Erie Lowlands, Blue Ridge region, Atlantic Coastal Plain, and New England Uplands make up smaller portions of the state's geography.

Pennsylvania is a mountainous state. The Appalachian Ridge and Valley region sweeps across the state from the northeast to the southwest. Deep valleys, jagged mountains, and thick forests cover the Appalachians. The region's Mount Davis is the highest point in the state. It rises 3,213 feet (979 m) above sea level.

Northwestern Pennsylvania's Allegheny Plateau is made up of narrow valleys and high, flat plateaus. The land there contains rich deposits of natural resources. Coal and natural gas are both mined to use as fuel to heat homes.

From the Appalachians (opposite) to the Alleghenies (above), Pennsylvania's land is marked by mountains and widespread forests.

YEAR
1787   The U.S. Constitution is written in Philadelphia, and Pennsylvania becomes the second state on December 12.
EVENT

- 13 -

Pennsylvania fields

Cherry orchard

Rolling plains and low hills make up the landscape of the Piedmont in southeastern Pennsylvania. Farms in the Piedmont produce potatoes, vegetables, and mushrooms. Pennsylvania grows more mushrooms than any other state.

The Erie Lowlands are found in the northwestern corner of the state along Lake Erie. This region produces grapes and potatoes. Southern Pennsylvania's Blue Ridge region is hilly and dotted with fruit orchards and dairy farms.

A small corner of southeastern Pennsylvania, known as the Atlantic Coastal Plain, is filled with marshes and small streams. Just north of the Plain are the New England Uplands. A narrow finger of forested land, the New England Uplands border the Delaware River.

The cherry orchards of south-central Pennsylvania (opposite) and the farm fields of the southeast (above) help provide fruit and grains to the entire region.

Thick, green forests cover three-fifths of Pennsylvania's land area. Among the dark green pines, leafy elms, and sprawling oak trees are native flowering plants such as rhododendrons. White-tailed deer and black bears roam the woods. Other animals such as red and gray foxes, coyotes, and bobcats are also found in Pennsylvania.

White-tailed deer are a common sight in the many wooded areas throughout Pennsylvania.

More than 4,500 rivers and streams flow from the mountains into the low-lying areas of Pennsylvania. Both the Delaware River and the Susquehanna River flow east to the Atlantic. The Allegheny and Monongahela rivers meet in Pittsburgh to form the great Ohio River.

Pennsylvania has hundreds of lakes. Most of the lakes were formed when dams were built on the state's rivers. Raystown Lake is the largest lake within state borders. In the north, Lake Erie provides a means of transportation for goods traveling to and from Pennsylvania. Ships sail from Lake Erie and through the St. Lawrence Seaway to reach the Atlantic Ocean.

Lake Arthur, in Moraine State Park, is a good place to fish for largemouth bass and bluegill.

Pennsylvania summers are warm and wet, and winters are cold and snowy. The mountainous areas experience cooler temperatures than the lowlands. Weather patterns change quickly in Pennsylvania, as winds off Lake Erie can bring strong storms and snow. The state averages 42 inches (107 cm) of precipitation a year.

YEAR

1793 An outbreak of yellow fever kills approximately 5,000 people in Philadelphia.

EVENT

A Place to Stay

William Penn made the Pennsylvania colony a welcome place for all European settlers. Germans, Swiss, and English were some of the first to settle in the area. People of many different religious beliefs came to Pennsylvania. The region's early settlers were a combination of Mennonites, Quakers, Amish, Brethren, and Roman Catholics.

Coal companies employed both those who could mine and those who could sort through the rocks using conveyor belts.

Many of these first settlers farmed for a living. Others lived in Philadelphia, where they worked at printing presses, made horseshoes, or owned taverns and inns. Later, many immigrants from Ireland, Italy, and eastern Europe came to work in Pennsylvania's mills, mines, and factories.

Today, many Pennsylvanians are employed in the tourism industry. They work as tour guides in historic places or as rangers in Pennsylvania's many forests and parks. Some Pennsylvanians still farm for a living or work in mines in the western part of the state.

In the cities, many people work in restaurants, hotels, and shops. Other city dwellers work with computer technology and in education. Steel manufacturing has declined since its boom in the early 20th century, but the food-processing

Amish people have lived and farmed near Lancaster, Pennsylvania, for almost 300 years.

YEAR

1863 The Battle of Gettysburg stops the South's advance into the North, turning the tide of the Civil War.

EVENT

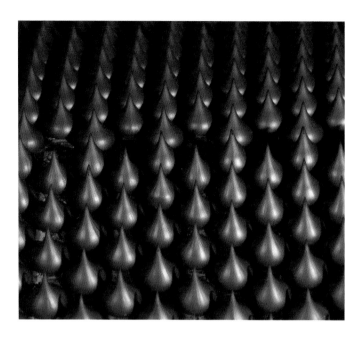

industry has enjoyed steady growth. Food-processing plants, such as the Hershey Company in Hershey and H. J. Heinz in Pittsburgh, employ thousands of workers.

Most Pennsylvanians today are white. African Americans make up about 10 percent of the population. Hispanic and Asian Americans are the next largest groups. Only a small number of American Indians still live in Pennsylvania. About 85 percent of Pennsylvanians live in the state's larger cities such as Pittsburgh and Philadelphia.

The Pennsylvania Dutch are a unique group of Pennsylvanians. During colonial times, the Pennsylvania Dutch spoke German, or Deutsch, and were called "Dutch" by other colonists. Today, about 50,000 Pennsylvania Dutch live in the southeastern part of the state. Some still speak a mixture of English and German. Many live simply. Some Pennsylvania Dutch, such as the Amish, do not use cars or electricity. Other Pennsylvania Dutch groups include Mennonites, Moravians, and Brethren.

About 215 miles (346 km) east of Pittsburgh (opposite), Hershey's Kisses are produced at the famous chocolate factory (above).

Pennsylvania has been home to many famous people. Betsy Ross was a famous early colonist who lived in Philadelphia. Some stories say that she made the very first American flag in 1776. Ross also made flags for Pennsylvania's navy during the Revolutionary War. A major Philadelphia bridge is named in her honor.

Another famous Pennsylvania woman was Mary Cassatt. Cassatt was a painter in the late 1800s. She studied painting at the Pennsylvania Academy of the Fine Arts in Philadelphia. She then moved to France and was associated with other artists known as Impressionists.

A 19th-century painting of Betsy Ross sewing the first American flag (above) and Mary Cassatt's Mother and Child, *1893 (opposite), show very different styles.*

1902   Large-scale strikes in Pennsylvania mines increase public support for miners and the United Mine Workers Union.

Bill Cosby is a well-known comedian from Philadelphia. His television series, *The Cosby Show,* was a popular comedy about African American family life. Famous actress Grace Kelly was also from Philadelphia. She starred in many films during the 1950s. When she married a prince from the country of Monaco, she became known as "Princess Grace."

Many people who visit Pennsylvania decide to stay and make it their home. They are drawn in by the state's exciting cities, lovely mountains, and career opportunities. Studies show that most people who were born in Pennsylvania choose to live and work in the state their entire lives. A forest, a mountain, or a piece of history is often right outside their back doors.

Unlike Grace Kelly, who went from an acting career to becoming royalty (opposite), Bill Cosby (above) was always a performer.

YEAR

1920   The first commercial radio station in the U.S. broadcasts from Pittsburgh.

EVENT

- 25 -

Pennsylvania Pride

IN PENNSYLVANIA, THERE IS HISTORY IN EVERY STEP.
PHILADELPHIA'S INDEPENDENCE PARK IS THE FIRST
STOP FOR MANY VISITORS TO THE "CITY OF BROTHERLY
LOVE." ON THE GROUNDS OF THE PARK IS INDEPENDENCE
HALL. NOT FAR FROM INDEPENDENCE HALL STANDS
THE LIBERTY BELL. THE CRACKED BELL IS A SYMBOL OF
AMERICAN FREEDOM.

Southwest of Philadelphia is a landmark that represents another struggle for freedom. Gettysburg National Military Park honors soldiers who died during the bloody Civil War battle. Visitors can tour the battlefield on horseback, watch a reenactment of the fighting, and even stand where President Lincoln gave his powerful speech.

Northeast of Gettysburg, Lancaster County is true Pennsylvania Dutch country. There, cars and trucks share the road with Amish horse-drawn buggies. Amidst the farms is the town of Lancaster, where visitors can indulge in hearty Pennsylvania Dutch food such as chicken and dumplings, chicken potpie, and pancakes. Handmade quilts are a popular item to buy in Lancaster. The colorful quilts are decorated with such traditional images as hearts, tulips, and birds.

The town of Hershey is a popular destination for chocolate lovers. The streets are lined with streetlights in the shape of Hershey's Kisses, and the sweet smell of chocolate is always in the air. The Hershey factory, where Milton Hershey began making chocolate in 1905, churns out delicious candy every day. Hershey was one of the first to mix milk with cocoa to make sweet milk chocolate, and Americans have loved Hershey's chocolate ever since.

Pennsylvania tourists can visit the Liberty Bell (opposite) and watch people act out important Civil War battles (above).

YEAR

1979   An accident occurs at Three Mile Island nuclear power plant near Middletown and releases harmful radiation.

EVENT

Every year on February 2, visitors crowd the streets of the small town of Punxsutawney in central Pennsylvania. They come to see its most famous resident, Punxsutawney Phil, the country's official weather-predicting groundhog. On Groundhog Day, Phil emerges from his hole. The people in the crowd hold their breath, wondering if he will see his shadow. Popular legend holds that if Phil sees his shadow, there will be six more weeks of winter.

No matter the weather, Pennsylvanians always have their favorite sports teams to keep them busy. The state has two professional football teams, the Philadelphia Eagles and the Pittsburgh Steelers. The Philadelphia Flyers and the Pittsburgh Penguins are Pennsylvania's professional hockey teams. The Philadelphia Phillies and the Pittsburgh Pirates play major league baseball, and the Philadelphia 76ers play pro basketball. At the college level, Pennsylvania State's championship-winning football team doesn't disappoint its legions of fans across the country.

Along with watching sporting events, experiencing nature is a popular Pennsylvania pastime. The Delaware Water Gap, on the border of Pennsylvania and New Jersey, draws

Punxsutawney Phil (above) and Pittsburgh Steelers quarterback Ben Roethlisberger (opposite) are two of the state's most famous newsmakers.

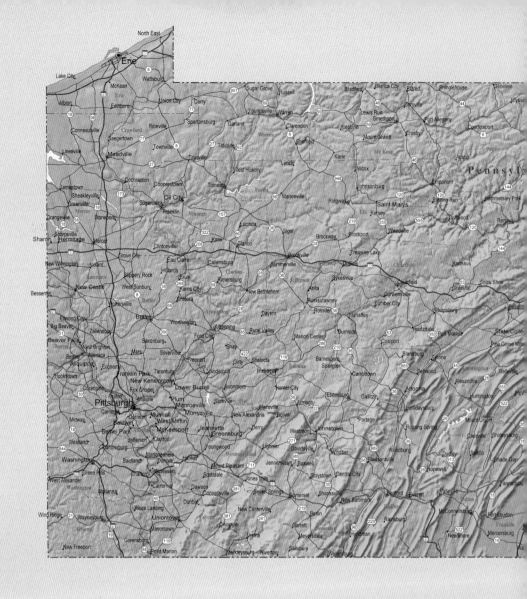

QUICK FACTS

Population: 12,432,792

Largest city: Philadelphia (pop. 1,449,634)

Capital: Harrisburg

Entered the union: December 12, 1787

Nickname: Keystone State

State flower: mountain laurel

State bird: ruffed grouse

Size: 46,055 sq mi (119,282 sq km)—33rd-biggest in U.S.

Major industries: tourism, manufacturing, farming, mining

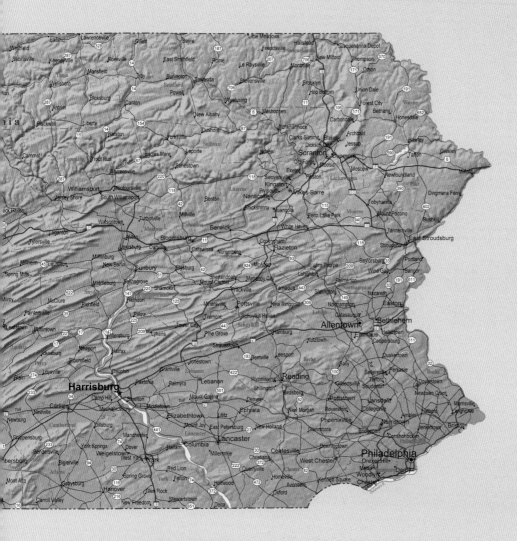

thousands of tourists each year. The gap was formed when the Delaware River sliced through a mountain ridge 1,000 feet (305 m) high. Visitors can swim at the area's many beaches, go fishing or hiking, or just marvel at the beauty of the region.

A lush land filled with deep history, Pennsylvania has been nicknamed "The Keystone State." A keystone is the central stone in an arch that helps hold all the other stones in place. America's founding fathers developed their ideas of liberty and equality in Pennsylvania, making the state deserving of such an important name. As Pennsylvania's people move into the future, they take pride in knowing that their state remains the keystone of the country.

YEAR
2001
EVENT

On September 11, a plane taken over by terrorists crashes near Shanksville, Pennsylvania.

- 31 -

BIBLIOGRAPHY

Commonwealth of Pennsylvania. "Pennsylvania: State of Independence." Pennsylvania State Government. http://www.pa.gov/portal/server.pt.

Miller, Joanne. *Moon Handbooks: Pennsylvania*. Emeryville, Calif.: Avalon Travel, 2005.

O'Toole, Christine. *Off the Beaten Path: Pennsylvania*. Guilford, Conn.: Globe Pequot Press, 2007.

Root, Douglas. *Compass American Guides: Pennsylvania*. New York: Compass American Guides, 2003.

Walter, Eugene. *The Smithsonian Guides to Natural America: The Mid-Atlantic States—New York, Pennsylvania, and New Jersey*. Washington, D.C.: Smithsonian Books, 1996.

INDEX